W0005956
THIS FUCKTIONARY BELONG TO:

A review on Amazon
would be amazing!

Fucktionary: A bad word coloring book for adults only!

Printed by Amazon KDP
First Printing, 2020

Graphic design and illustration by ©2020 Mahsa Memarzadeh

ISBN: 9798577885809

Shitastrophy
(n.)
Word used for massive mess ups, fucked up situations, & epic fails.

Askhole (n.)
A person who constantly asks for your advice, yet always does the opposite of what you told them.

Ignoranus
(adj)
Someone who
is both stupid
& asshole!

Multitasking
(n.)
SCREWING
several things
AT THE SAME TIME!

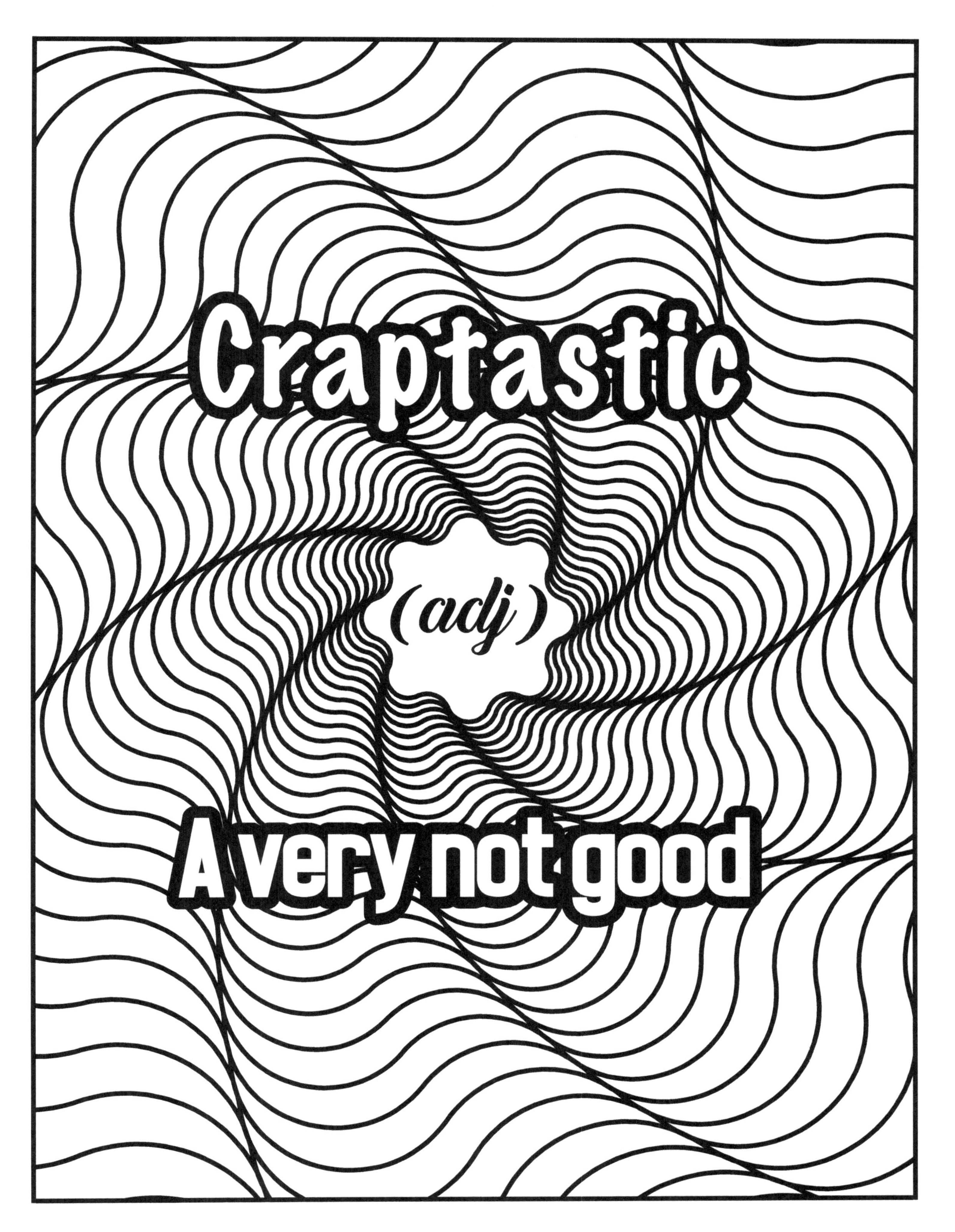
Craptastic
(adj)
A very not good

WTF
(phr.)
Where's
the
food?

Chestickes (n.)
When you're an
amazing, brave, take
no shit goddess & got
more serious balls
but
they're on your chest!

Home
(n.)
Where you
trust the toilet seat!

FUCK
The only
fucking word
that can be put
every fucking where
&
still fucking make
fucking sense.

When the urge to make a **SARCASTIC REPLY** is so overwhelming *you can only* **roll your eyes and grunt incoherently!**

Slut (n.)
a woman
with the
morals of a
MAN

BADASS
(adj)
Someone who does not
ever, look back at an
explosion.

Bitch
(n.)
Any girl
who is prettier than
YOU!

NILLIONAIRE
(adj)
Someone
Having Little
to
No Money.
$

FARTLED
(v)
to be
startled
by a surprise or loud
FART.

Déjabrew
(n.)
Slowly remembering things you did while DRUNK.

THE FUCKENING
When your day is going
too well
but you don't
trust it
& some SHIT finally
GOES DOWN!

Ambitchous
(adj)
striving to be
more of a bitch
than the
AVERAGE
BITCH!

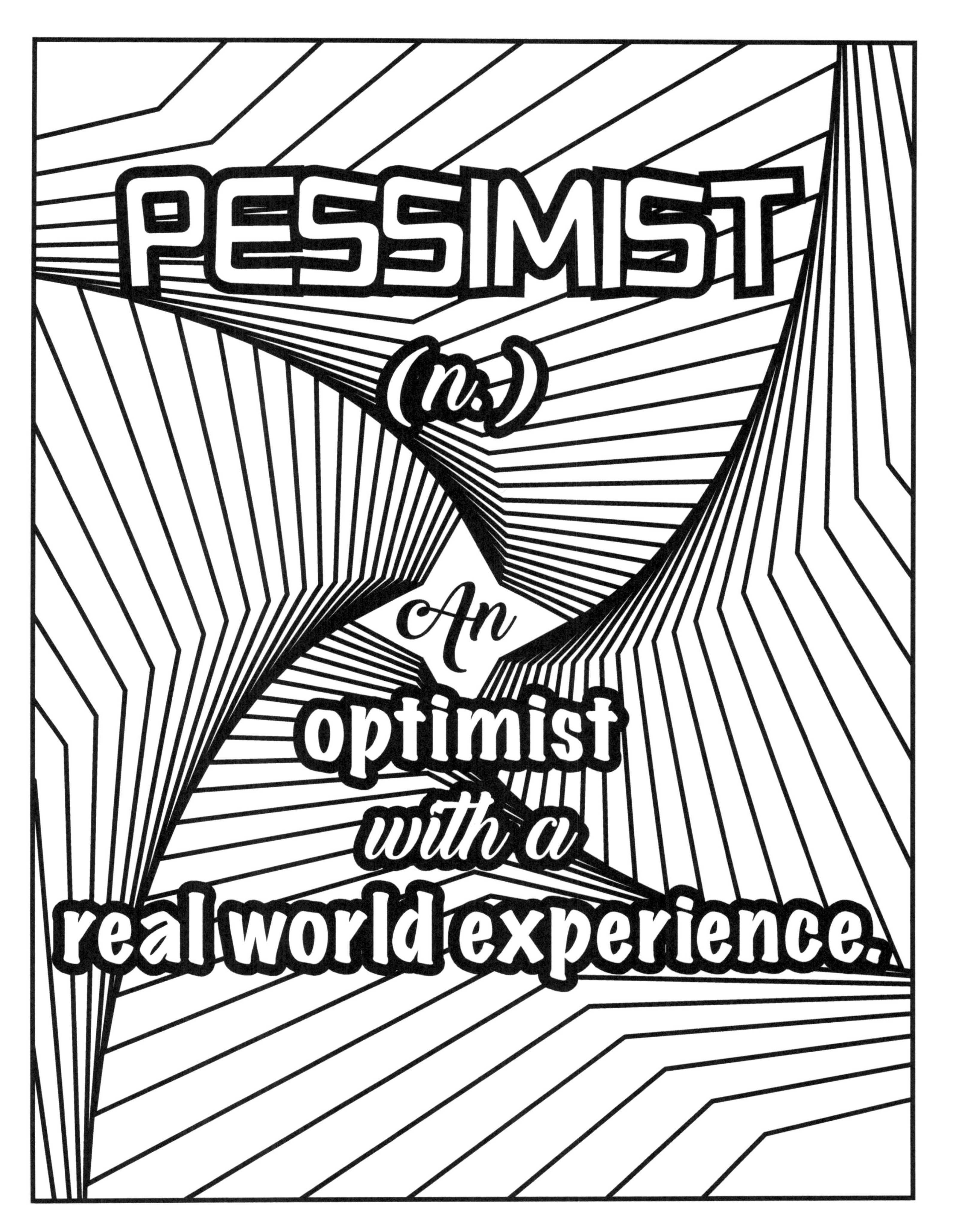
PESSIMIST
(n.)
An
optimist
with a
real world experience.

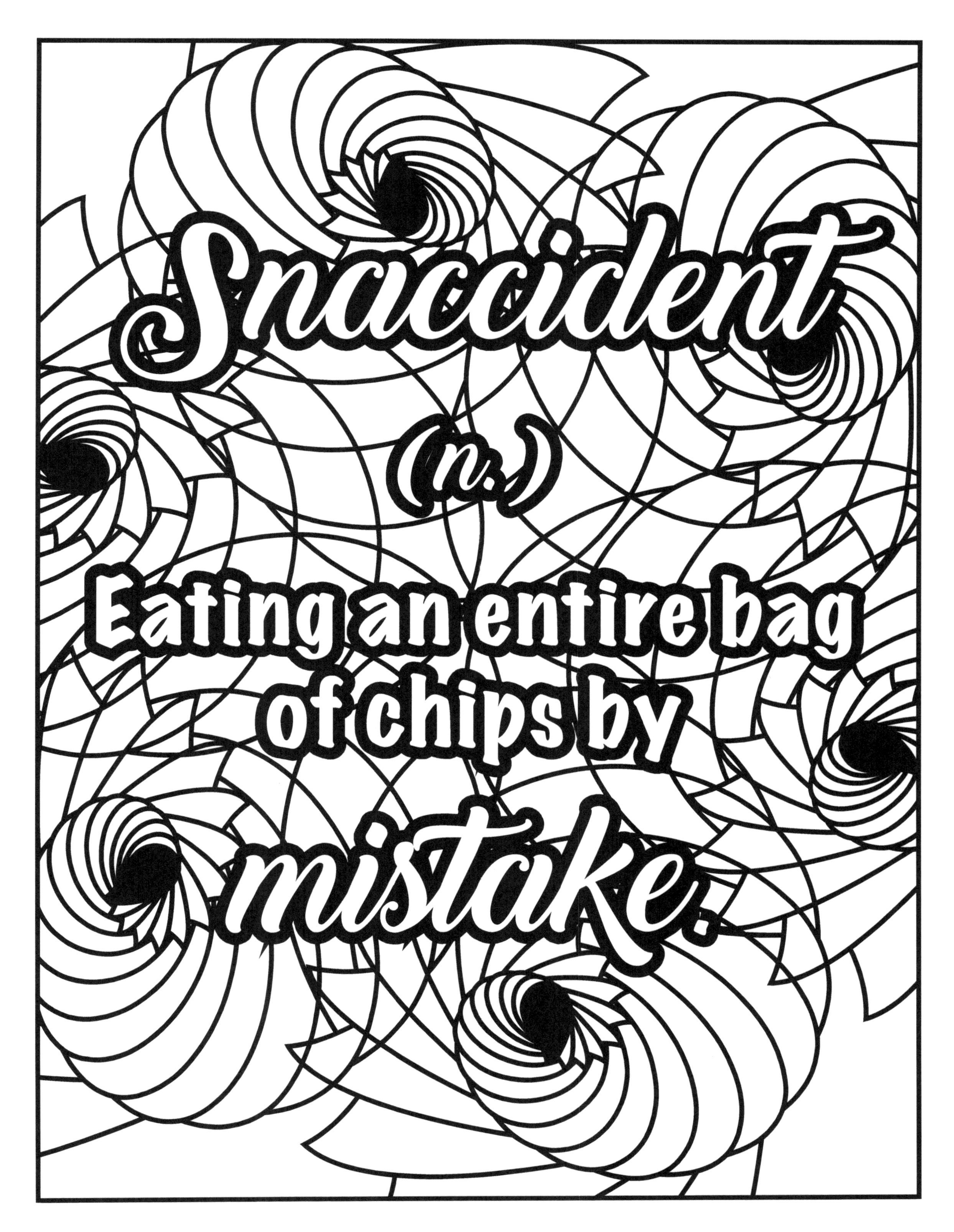
Snaccident
(n.)
Eating an entire bag
of chips by
mistake.

HANGRY
(adj)
When you are so
hungry
that your
lack of food
causes you to become
Angry, Frustrated or Both.

Cellfish
(adj)
People who just
focus on their phones
when they're hanging
out with you.

MOMSTER
(n.)
What happens to
MOM
after she counts to three.

Déjapoo
(n.)
The feeling that you've
heard this
CRAP
before.

BEDGASM
(n.)
The feeling of
euphoria you get
when lying down
in your bed
after a very long day.

VODKA
(n.)
A drink
which makes you
STRONGER
& CLEVER

Pornocchio
(n.)
A person who embellishes
their sex life
in order to sound cooler.

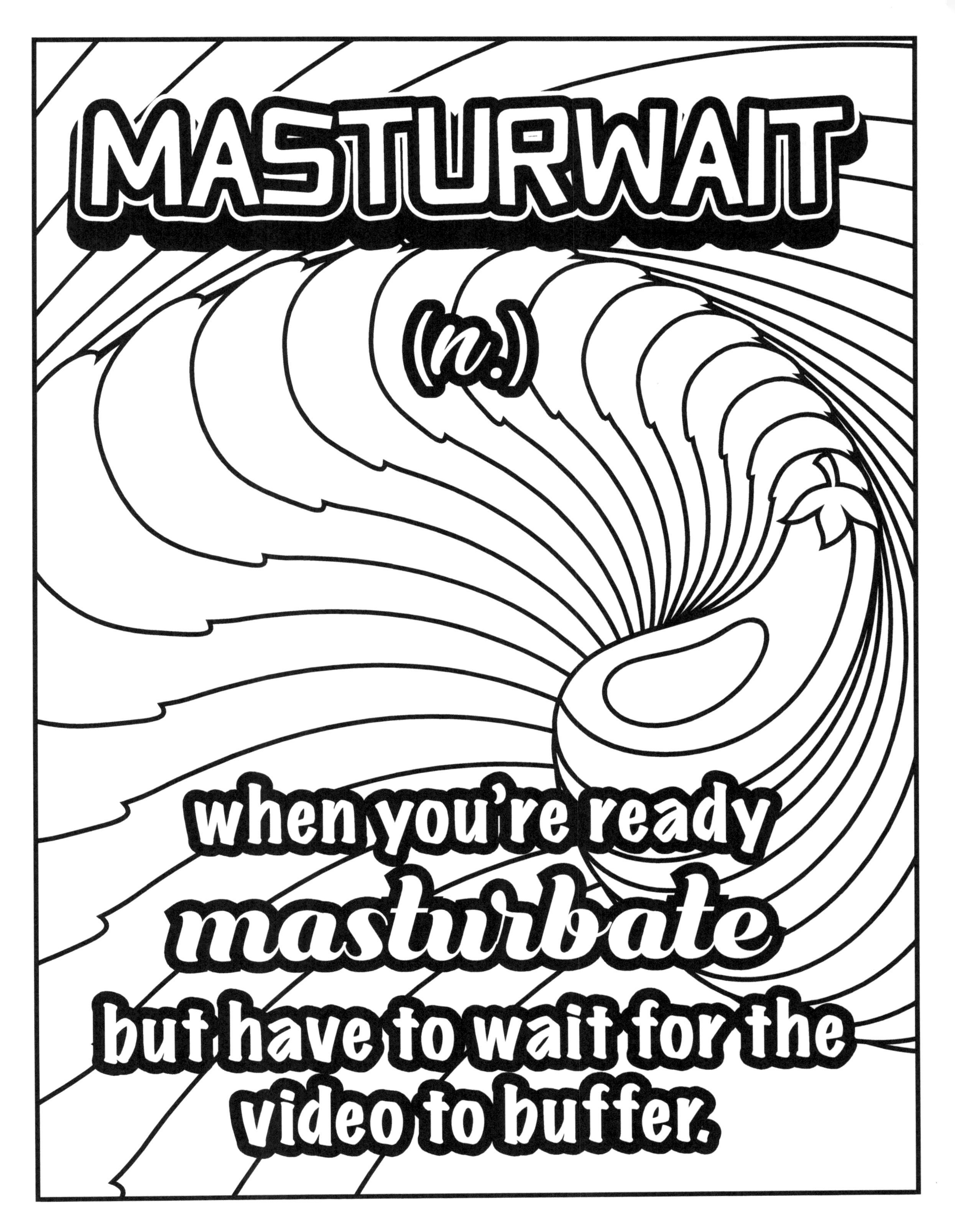
MASTURWAIT
(n.)
when you're ready
masturbate
but have to wait for the
video to buffer.

Condomplate
(v)
to contemplate the use
of a condom.

FLAWSOME
(adj)
An individual who embraces their flaws and knows they are awesome regardless.

Printed in the USA
CPSIA information can be obtained
at www.ICGtesting.com
LVHW081518061224
798539LV00037B/1283

* 9 7 9 8 5 7 7 8 8 5 8 0 9 *